PSALMS THAT HALLOW THE SABBATH

PSALMS THAT HALLOW THE SABBATH

NORMAN M. CHANSKY

RESOURCE *Publications* • Eugene, Oregon

PSALMS THAT HALLOW THE SABBATH

Resource Publications
An Imprint of Wipf and Stock Publishers
199 W. 8th Ave., Suite 3
Eugene, OR 97401

www.wipfandstock.com

PAPERBACK ISBN: 978-1-5326-6288-1
HARDCOVER ISBN: 978-1-5326-6289-8
EBOOK ISBN: 978-1-5326-6290-4

Manufactured in the U.S.A.   10/02/18

To my readers:
God Has Been my muse. I am your scribe. I invite you to be
my voice.

Acknowledgements

SABBATH! THE WORD ROUSES relief in many a heart. After a week of labor, workers feel free to relax and pursue what they dreamed about all week. The Sabbath was mandated in the old Testament as a day of rest, God Rested on the seventh day of Creation. Not just an ordinary day but a holy day. In fact, "Keep the Sabbath" is a commandment that Moses brought down from Mount Sinai. Work was proscribed. Jesus Relaxed the command. He cited King David who is said to have told his hungry companions on The Sabbath to eat the shew bread, one baked from the finest of flour.

The Sabbath In the Jewish tradition and the Eastern Orthodox tradition is celebrated on Saturday. The Moslem holy day is Friday. Buddhists also observe a holy day. It is not only a day to abstain from work but a day filled with joy. This collection of poems contains verses that portray several scintillating facets of the Sabbath. They glorify the day and make it holy. The Sabbath is a gem filled with more luster than a pearl, more colorful than a rainbow, more precious than rubies, more scintillating than gold, more uplifting than songs of joy or paintings by the Masters, and more stirring than a military march. It is a class by itself and defies comparisons. It is a day of beauty, splendor, elegance, and, above all, Grace.

I dedicate this collection to my wife Elissa Ruth, a blessing to us all, to our children: Linda, James, Keren, Tamar, and Matthew; to our grandchildren: Elizabeth Rachel, Sara, Bethany, Allison,

Isaac, Gilad, Kinneret, Meredith, Raia, and Emma; and to our great grandchildren, Daniella, Eitan, Arran, Rona, Nadav, and Eleanor. What blessings they are.

This collection of poems honors The Sabbath, a Sacred Time of rest and renewal Decreed by God. The Sabbath is a legacy from my parents. Theirs was a bequest from their ancestors. I pass on my inheritance to friends and family of now and those yet to be. The verses reach deep into the depths of our souls and awaken reverent feelings we gather during the week. Not only do these variations on a theme delve into the deep crevices of our souls but uplift, dignify, enhance, and ennoble us. The Sabbath is a sparkling gem in the history of Time.

Its facets are many; its sheen glosses our lives. The poems presented here reflect the unique, exquisite, and diverse aspects of The Sabbath. Peoples throughout the world celebrate The Sabbath in ways schooled by their cultural lore. Many with song and prayer; others with dance. It is a time to exhale from daily breathtaking efforts, primp and preen, and sit at a table, graced with delectable foods, surrounded by loving friends and family. It is a time to honor the past and hope for a benevolent future. It is a time to express our thanks for the bounty we enjoy. It is time that envelops us in gratitude and serenity. It is our connection with the past and with the future.

Introduction

PASSING ON A LEGACY

Sing unto God a new song; all the earth sing unto God. Sing unto God, bless The Name; proclaim salvation every day.—Ps 96

THE SABBATH: ZENITH OF THE WEEK

The Bible says that on the seventh day of Creation God Invested with holiness, a time of respite from Creation's endeavors. Gen 2:3 God Rested on the seventh day and made it holy. Throughout time we have invested in the Sabbath a sacred day of rest and renewal, an island of tranquility 'mid turbulent tides'. It is a haven to all. It is a time to steer our voyage through life into a secure harbor and lower our anchor. Just as God Rested on the Sabbath, we are bidden to become at ease on that day. Behold the radiant Sabbath Sovereign, Envoy of God, Reigning over all seeking refuge from the ordinary and mundane. Embracing every soul on the placid island with Divine Love, and adorning every heart with God's Wisdom, Justice, and Joy. Holding high is a beacon, a lamp to guide our way to a better life.

Norman Chansky, PH.D.
Professor Emeritus, Temple University

1. THE GLORIES OF CREATION

CONSIDER THE MARVEL AND delight of Creation, The iridescent glow of the sapphire; the tints and tones of the rainbow; the melodic songs of the birds; the fixed rhythm of the seasons; the daily tempo of the Earth about the golden sun; the pure joy of the Sabbath, a day to notice what is magnificent and sublime in the Cosmos. A day to give thanks for the beauty bestowed.

2. THE ANGELS SING A SACRED ANTHEM

Now is the hour to greet the Sabbath. Angels Sing an anthem to God's Creation. They coax the Holy Spirit to ascend to the most Exalted Eminence of Divinity. Join and praise the Compassionate Guardian of the frail. Join God in making this a safer, happier world.

3. SABBATH DAY: GOD'S BLESSINGS OF BLISSFUL LOVE

On the Sabbath Angels Arrive on wings of a dove to bring God's Blessings of blissful love. Praised be God. Hallelujah.

4. SABBATH: A TIME OF GLADNESS

The curtain of Sabbath rises and reveals a Sacred Time of Gladness; a hallowed Time of Mirth; a Time to rejoice in the magnificence of the World's Birth; a venerated Time to reflect on the Gift of Selfhood; a devout Time to consecrate our souls to what is noble and good.

5. SABBATH: AWAKENING OF THE SENSES

On the Sabbath our ears hearken to songs birds sing. Our eyes behold the brilliance of flowers; our hearts pulse with the rhythm of the universe; our minds ponder the beauty of Creation; our souls embrace the Benevolence of the Divine Embrace.

6. BEAR WITNESS TO THE SABBATH

What a miracle it is one day each week to bear witness to the Sabbath. How blessed we are to sow Sabbath Joy; how happy are we to reap Sabbath peace; what a delight it is to be embraced by Angels—God's Envoys. How Blessed are we to reap the serenity of Sabbath Peace.

7. WE GIVE THANKS FOR GOD'S WONDERS

We give thanks for wonders we witnessed this past week. We give thanks for the beauty God Divine Bestows. Come greet the Sabbath. Peer at your soul and behold the glow of God's Grandeur.

8. BURNISH THE SABBATH WITH PSALM, SONG, AND DANCE

Pause from the daily routine to usher in the day of peace and healing for which all yearn. Burnish its luster with psalm, with song, with dance.

9. CLASP HANDS TO PROCLAIM THAT PEACE CAN GROW

Sabbath Day Is here. Let's clasp hands in love to show the watching world that peace can grow. Let's cast aside affronts of yore and cherish one another forever more. Join together in sacred song. In harmony alone free joy from the Eternal Spring to teach everyone how to sing.

Send rhythm from Your Vast Expanse to teach us how to dance. Invite Sabbath Angels to teach us how to bring delight.

10. SABBATH: ZENITH OF THE WEEK

Our parents, like those who preceded them, opened our eyes to the radiance which the Sabbath Day beams.

The Sabbath is the jewel in the crown of Creation.

11. THE SABBATH GILDS OUR LIVES WITH GOLDEN DREAMS

How good it is to dwell among smiling faces. The Sabbath is the time that banishes anguish. It is the day that tints our lives with golden dreams and silver hopes.

12. GRANT US THE VISION TO SEE THE GOOD IN OTHERS

The sun o'er the tree crown fades from view And daubs the skies a crimson hue. Oh God! Grant us vision to see the good others do. Grant us wisdom to understand Your world. Grant us laughter to soften our loads. This Sabbath Spread Your peace throughout our abodes.

14. IT IS SABBATH: AWAKE SLEEPING ANGELS

Awake Sleeping Angels to the sun's afterglow. Families await You in their homes below with Garlands of Blessings our souls to adorn. Once again on the Sabbath will we be reborn.

15. HEAVENLY ANGELS APPEAR TO US ON THE SABBATH

On Sabbath eve we contemplate where we have been, where we are and where we are going. Heavenly Angels Appear to us in a bower of sweet dreams and Surround us with exquisite thoughts of joy, glistening with Divine Radiance.

16. THE SABBATH UNFOLDS DEEP IN OUR BREASTS

This week has run its course to greet weeks past alive in our minds. Beyond mothers and fathers and children it winds through eons of history to its Divine Source. The Sabbath unfolds deep in our breasts shining its Light our souls to renew. It Fills us with Blessings our lives to imbue and enfolds us with joy at God's Behest.

17. IT IS THE SABBATH AND WE WASH OUR WORRIES AWAY

As The Sabbath draws nigh we wash our worries away and prepare to don the raiment of Sabbath peace and from our cares seek release.

18. ON THE SABBATH WE WRAP OURSELVES IN JOY

At dusk the once turquoise sky becomes flecks of pink and grey. Sabbath unfolds from Its Heavenly cocoon, Spiraling into our breasts, agleam with Divine Grace. It fastens to our souls and we become partners in rejuvenating God's Creation.

19. WRAP OURSELVES IN SABBATH JOY

Let's wrap ourselves in Sabbath joy and feel its warm embrace. Let's open our eyes to the wonders of God's Creation, and thank our forbears for protecting them.

20. DRAW THE CURTAIN ON THIS WEEK'S WORRIES

Fasten the curtains on this week's worries. Secure the gates to the mundane. It is Sabbath, a time to heal and an hour to open the portal to the holy.

21. THE SABBATH IS FILLED WITH WONDER AND BEAUTY

A prayer shawl wraps the Sabbath with wonder and beauty. Our hearts are brimming with merriment and joy. How filled is the Sabbath with calm and tranquility. How brimming over it is with Grandeur and Nobility.

22. SABBATH ARRIVES IN THE SILENCE OF DUSK

In the stillness of dusk Sabbath arrives crowning our souls with gladness, giving hope to the oppressed, healing to the infirm, comfort the grieving, and enveloping all with Joy Divine.

23. SABBATH: APOGEE OF THE WEEK

This week crests toward its apogee and coalesces with eons of history. Ruby, emerald, and coral plumes bejewel the evening sky; vestiges of the golden orb dazzle the eye. Heavenly harps strum and Celestial voices hum their welcome to the Sabbath Sovereign: hallowed presence, beauty verdant and carmine.

24. SABBATH SPREADS DOLLOPS OF JOY

Wrinkled clouds swirl slowly 'neath a purple mantled sky. The Sabbath is nigh spreading, dollops of joy to raise the spirits of a melancholy world.

25. ENFOLD YOURSELF IN THE SABBATH CLOAK

Enfold yourself in the The Sabbath Shawl, a Gift of God, to enthrall the world. Invite its Spirit to enchant your soul. Savor its solace, joy, contentment, and healing. Bask in the Divine Radiant Gift.

26. A CUPFUL OF SABBATH AS THE WEEK CLOSES

A cupful of SABBATH as the week comes to a close puts smiles on our faces and peace bestows, puts hope in our hearts and casts out despair, fashions sweet dreams and banishes care, sings songs to the soul from sacred time antique, does a cupful of Sabbath at the close of the week.

27. BEHOLD THE SABBATH SOVEREIGN APPROACHES

Behold the Sabbath Sovereign approaches, Draped in regal splendor our lives to beautify. Draw closer to The Sabbath Presence, Burnish our souls till it gleams and glows, And peace and joy within us grows.

28. THE GOLDEN SUN SLOWLY FADES IN THE WEST

The golden sun slowly fades, and crimson clouds pink the Western sky. As on every Sabbath throughout the years, we count the ways we've been Blessed.

29. SABBATH WRAPS US IN SWEET EMBRACE

Sabbath arrives wrapping all in its embrace, Blessing us with soundness of body, serenity of soul, and wisdom of mind.

30. SABBATH ENVELOPS US IN THE SACRED

Sabbath arrives enveloping us in holiness. Blessing us with all that is sacred.

31. THIS SABBATH WE ASCEND TO THE HEIGHTS OF THE MOST HIGH

As Sabbath grows nigh and the week's labor is at an end, we ascend to the heights of the most high to embrace the Holy One, our Special Friend. There in the midst of Sacred Space where a gentle zephyr blows, cloaked are we in Heavenly Grace and serenity within us glows.

32. WELCOME SABBATH: SOURCE OF LIGHT

Welcome Sabbath source of light whose celestial radiance by God is blessed. Release us from our daily plight; Guide us in our peaceful quest. Help us climb to heights sublime that renew our souls so bare, Sabbath is a Paradigm of Lambent Joy for everyone to share.

33. SABBATH: RESPLENDENT DIADEM

Sabbath Day, resplendent diadem, draws near burnished by our ardent prayers, crowns our souls with serenity and inspires each of us to become the soul we seek to be.

34. THE PAST WEEK OF TOIL IS HISTORY

The past week of toil has passed into history. Etched in our memories are shadows of trials and echoes of our triumphs. Looming behind the pale clouds of the ordinary is the beaming light of Sabbath sent from Heaven to bathe us in serenity.

35. SABBATH: A TIME TO PAUSE FROM WEEKLY CHORES

Sabbath has come and week's work is done. Everyone pauses from last week's duties. Oceans wash the golden sun, unveiling hues of orange and pink. Fringes of night blanket the sky. Without notice atoms escape and spin away from the Sacred Source toward every yearning soul, toward God's Love they course.

36. SABBATH: SHINING CROWN

Sabbath—shining crown, climax of the week! A day of rest when all labor ends and thoughts turn to how richly we are blessed. We exult in The Sabbath: holy day of rest.

37. SABBATH: A TIME FOR SOLITUDE

Deep inside the interior of Sabbath: is solitude, a quiet moment to coalesce with God's Infinitude, and sip at the font of Providence and listen to The voice of the Divine spiraling in silence. Then Sabbath: makes us its friend; Then will our souls toward serenity wend.

38. SCARLET FEATHERS SPREAD ACROSS THE SKY

Scarlet feathers spread across the dusky sky. The sun is setting as Sabbath draws nigh. We gather near family praying that a tiara of peace will crown all on this sacred day. Candles are kindled and flaming feathers leap and dance and fill the dark world with radiance. As our fingers circle the flames, we whisper blessings as ancestors before had spoken, "Blessed art thou who sanctifies Sabbath, Bless all children. May they grow to be honest and wise." That moment is holier than any instant we know. For the blessings received we bask in their glow.

39. SABBATH USHERS IN CELESTIAL BEAUTY

Dusk draws nigh, lavender ribbons ring the sky. The golden disc slips from view, Its celestial beauty was a wonder to behold. Then the curtains of Heaven open wide. There before us is The Sabbath: Sovereign, Bearer of hope, Herald of peace, Envoy of joy; Courier of health.

40. SABBATH: JUNCTION OF YESTERDAY AND TOMORROW

Sabbath Eve is the crossroads of yesterday and tomorrow, of despair and hope, of trial and calm, of sadness and solace, of pain and joy, of fault finding and forgiving, of the ordinary and the sacred. At the crux of the holy day we recall those whom we cherish, loved ones of today and those long gone who by their virtue still nourish us when we are alone. We beckon Angels to surround us with rest and to revive our weary bodies. Imbue us, we pray, with zest to savor Divine pleasures with rapture.

41. EARTH JOURNEYS ACROSS THE SKY

Earth journeys across the horizon bidding au revoir to the sun whose rays gleam through a lapis shawl, now erupting in fuchsia streaks in the evening sky. Mother kindles candles, compass of time to welcome a day of Holiness when grief dissolves and anguish ceases, and the peace of The Sabbath emerges from its Celestial Sanctuary Enveloping and transforming us to the persons we aspire to be.

42. SABBATH: GOD'S TREASURE

Since last Sabbath, by the command of the Holy One. The curtain comes down upon another week. The mystique of The Sabbath wraps us in its sacred shawl, and we see the Blessings God bestows upon us. How honored are we to celebrate this day.

43. THE GATES OF SABBATH OPEN

Amethyst loops swirl in the evening sky, golden flecks delight the eye. Slowly the earth drifts away from the golden orb, splinters of ancient suns sparkle in the newborn night. The Gates of The Sabbath ope and we hearken to the voices of Angels of peace that beckon to us.

44. FLIGHTS OF ANGELS WING US TO A DAY OF REST

The lowering sun in the purpling dusk appears in the horizon's west when God Sends flights of Angels to wing us toward a day of rest. "Sabbath Peace, Sabbath Peace." They sweetly sing and our souls enfold and wrap us in Celestial Healing to glorify us with Divine gifts manifold.

45. THE SABBATH CURTAIN COMES DOWN ON ANOTHER WEEK

The mystique of Sabbath wraps us in its sacred shawl, and we see the gifts God Bestowed upon us all. Heaven sent are we to celebrate this day. How truly blessed are we to walk in God's Way.

46. THE GATES OF SABBATH OPEN

The gates of Sabbath open wide. Divine Light flows and bathes us in God's Mercy, Healing, and Joy. Let's dwell among the Divine gifts of repose, joy, and healing our guides this week.

47. CANDLES ARE KINDLED AND WE ARE AT PEACE

Round and round the Earth has slowly spun In endless trek about the sun. Now as evening shadows fall, wrapping Earth in a dusky shawl, the remaining plumes of feathered light dissolve inside the ebon night. Welcome Sabbath by God Divinely Blessed Ordained for all a day of rest. Six days we've toiled and we have languished at life we've roiled and we have anguished. But now candles are kindled and all cares cease In our souls grows Sabbath peace. From every care are we freed. Living our lives by God's Sacred Creed, an answer to every human need.

48. SABBATH: A DAY OF HARMONY

Today is Sabbath; a day of goodwill and harmony; a day of re-dedication; a time of new beginnings. Although our fate is at times filled with ache, our sacred destiny is ours to make.

49. THE SABBATH QUEEN CLOAKED IN THE SUBLIME

The harsh edges of the past week melt at dusk. The radiant warmth of Sabbath, Monarch of peace, kindles joy in every soul. The Sabbath sovereign cloaked in The Sublime Crowns the week with beauty and grace, ringing us with God's Love.

50. GAYLY DOES GOD GARB THE CELESTIAL SPHERE

It is dusk, a time to usher in The Sabbath, a day of rest. The golden orb fades from view. The once glorious azure skies are changing to an emerald-copper hue. How radiantly God Garbs the celestial sphere to announce the Sabbath when joy replaces sorrow. Worries melt away as we for human welfare pray.

51. ON SABBATH WE HONOR CREATION'S BIRTH

On Sabbath we honor Creation's birth when God from all work had rested. We suspend our daily toils and from all cares are divested.

52. SABBATH: MYSTERIOUS MARVEL, WORK OF ART

Mysterious Marvel, work of art welcome Sabbath, Day of Rest Crowning Creation's sublime glory Which God Has graciously Blessed and we honor at The Creator's Behest.

53. WELCOME SABBATH WITH SONG

Welcome Sabbath we sing together. Welcome Sabbath Day we ardently pray that we nurture and reap the Peace that God Has Sown.

54. SABBATH IS THE GREATEST JOY OF ALL

When can joy be found? When feeling the ropes of falling rain, when battling the blowing wind, when freeing the soul from festering fret, when coming together with caring friends. But the greatest joy of all is celebrating the solace of The Sabbath Day.

55. SABBATH: WHEN WE ARE DIVINELY BLESSED

Night time clouds veil the amber sky. Gone from view is Heaven's golden eye. Sabbath draws nigh; a time for rest, a moment when all are Divinely Blessed. And in every praying mind a taste of Paradise, sweet and kind. Beguiled are we by Heavenly charms. Safe are we from untold harms. Welcome Sabbath! Welcome! We fervently pray.

56. THE SABBATH IS A SACRED BLESSING

The Sabbath is a sacred blessing, Flowering into sprays of love, Gifts of Grace from Heaven above. Hearken to the Angels melody. They enchant us with their harmony. They infuse us with healing and cheer, joy and happiness for all near and dear. With all humanity are we blending.

57. SABBATH HYMNS BLESS THE NOTES

Sabbath hymns bless the notes that solemnize the harmony of Nature's laws. On Sabbath Day bliss astounds. On Sabbath Day joy abounds.

58. SABBATH, SABBATH: DELIGHT TO THE SENSES

Sabbath, Sabbath: delight to the senses. Oh God! We pray. Fill our ears with Sabbath song, our eyes with Sabbath joy, our souls with Sabbath peace.

59. SABBATH DAY: DISTANT ECHOES OF CREATION'S GLORY

Surging from the wellsprings of our soul are distant echoes of the sixth day of Creation. Listen to Heavenly hosts chant praises to God, Their lyrics resound throughout our beings. They proclaim the coming of Sabbath, a day of rest. The day the Divine God Has Blessed.

60. SABBATH CLOAKS OUR SOULS IN THE SACRED

Sabbath arrives cloaking our souls in the sacred. We are transformed into the persons we aspire to be. Our deepest thoughts, dormant all week awaken, our minds, occupied with the paltry ordinary, now energize and focus on mending this faltering world. Our bodies, subjected to all manner of strains, heal themselves through the rest that God Ordained, and pledge to honor every element of Creation.

61. SABBATH BURNISHES OUR SACRED SOULS

Sabbath is here to burnish our sacred souls and release the gift of goodness becoming ripe within us during the past week.

62. SABBATH AND THE ANGELS SING

On Sabbath the Angels sing and bring us Greetings from God. They Invite us to join Them in their song and share with all God's endless Love.

63. ON SABBATH ANGELS FILL OUR SOULS

On Sabbath, the celestial curtain rises. Angels, God's Envoys, emerge to fill our lives with wisdom, healing, joy, and rest for on Sabbath all are Heavenly Blessed.

64. SABBATH: GIFT OF GOD

This is The Sabbath, Gift of God, our caring friend, our strength when we feel weak, our vigor when our spirits languish. When we reflect on the grandeur of Creation how mightily are we Blessed. We gather courage to renew ourselves at God's Behest.

65. SABBATH STILLS VEXING VOICE

It is Sabbath a time to still vexing voices of days long gone. Hearken to the words of The Merciful God. They mantle us like a prayer shawl. This is a time of rest, a time of healing, a time of renewal, a time of hope.

66. SABBATH RENEWS OUR DREAMS

Each week day coats our souls with dross stifling the good persons we seek to be.

67. SABBATH IS BORN AND OUR SPIRITS CLIMB

A copse of clouds drift slowly toward the West and blanket the sun so the world can rest. The blue of the sky no longer is seen and the leaves of the trees no long are green. This day has come to a glorious end and night in the West begins to wend. At this moment: sacred, serene. sublime we spawn The Sabbath and our spirits soar.

68. ON SABBATH WE ASCEND GOD'S SACRED MOUNT

Every Sabbath as we to our prayers tend, God's sacred mount we ascend. Reaching the timeworn craggy peak. We find the solace we ardently seek. At that very moment are we in awe seated in the presence of Almighty God. Wrapped together in fringed shawl, partners are we to humanity's call. With tablets of mandates for all to do, we descend The Mount with hope anew. And when we enter into SABBATH time enfolding us is peaceful rest sublime.

69. WELCOME SABBATH: TIME OF REST

Welcome Sabbath this week's crest. Welcome Sabbath time of rest. With longing for peace in every breast, exultant are we in our quest.

70. WE DELIGHT IN THE SABBATH GOD HAS BLESSED

Oh God! On this day we pray with deepest conviction. Give us this day Your Benediction. How we delight in Sabbath You Have Ordained, and the Peace time we have attained.

71. OH GOD LEAD US INTO YOUR REALM OF LIGHT

Oh God, on this Sabbath lead us into Your realm of light, Where serenity reigns and kindness prevails. Oh God! On This Sabbath lead us into Your domain of hope where happiness fuels and patience prevails.

72. OH GOD LEAD US INTO YOUR CIRCLE OF WISDOM.

Oh God! On this Sabbath lead us into Your circle of wisdom where beauty presides and bliss prevails.

73. PILGRIMS ARE WE IN SEARCH OF GOD'S TRUTH

Pilgrims are we set out to find God's Truth.On Sabbath the clouds that veil the mind are dispersed and we clearly see and are beguiled by God's path to Light. Bathed in that Light God's Truth is revealed.

74. ON SABBATH WE SAUNTER TOWARD THE SACRED

It is Sabbath. We, pilgrims in search of the Divine, amble from the mundane and approach the sacred. Greeted are we by Angels of serenity chanting the anthem, "peace unto all." At that moment we become the persons God Ordained us to be and become a faithful trustees according to God's sacred decree.

75. SABBATH: THE SUN SETS IN THE WESTERN SKY

Oh God! Abate the raucous noise of our pain and placate each grating brain. Oh God! On the Sabbath excite our sleeping senses with wisdom and delight. Oh God! Inspire our hearts with caring and with joy. Lift us out of the mundane and raise us to the sublime.

76. SABBATH IS HERE ENFOLDING US IN PEACE AND HEALING

The last shafts of sunshine slip 'neath the horizon painting the evening sky a golden hue. Sabbath is here, enfolding us with peace and healing, our weary souls to renew.

77. SABBATH QUEST TO PRESERVE GOD'S CREATION

On Sabbath we persist at the quest to preserve God's Creation. We do homage to You through Your ordained Sabbath rest. Friend and strength in our frailties we honor You with silent strains in our souls.

78. SABBATH: INFINITE MOMENT IN TIME

This is Sabbath, an infinite moment of ecstasy in the biography of Time. A boundless moment of peace in the geography of Space. At this very moment I rivet my soul to you, The Creator.

79. SERENITY RINGS US ON SABBATH

Swirls of serenity surround us on Sabbath beckoning them to still the daily stresses that harass us. Bid them to replace with Divine Peace and Godly Grace the routine concerns that distress our minds. Then will we be Transformed into sacred children of the Almighty; then will we fill the hollows of the universe with songs of joy and delight.

80. OH GOD! YOU SOWED DIVINE SEEDS IN MY SOUL

Oh God of Mercy You Planted Divine seeds in my soul that sprout into compassion. With Wisdom, You sowed seeds of knowledge that grow into profound understanding. With Brilliance You created Sabbath that we may thrive with joy. How restored will we be.

81. SABBATH: GIFT OF GOD

Sabbath is a gift from God, wrapped in ribbons of love. It is a gift to share in joy, in rest, in prayer. When we invite the Sabbath spirit to embrace our souls, Serenity, flower of the Heavenly, adorns our lives.

82. SING WITH ZEST

Raise your voices and sing to honor The Sabbath Day of rest that God with Grace Blessed.

83. SING WITH SPIRIT

Oh Sabbath spirit, come to us from your abode; Guide us with your good will; Dwell in our souls; Release the rapture that abides within us; Free the serenity slumbering in our souls; Transform us into the elegant people that we are.

84. DEAR GOD! PLACE US 'NEATH THE SABBATH CANOPY

Dear God! Enfold us and place us 'neath the Sabbath canopy of tranquility arriving from its holy abode. Invite its spirit to enchant our souls, and savor its solace joy, contentment, and healing.

85. GOLDEN WAS THE DAY

Golden was the day and now at dusk a purple majesty ceils the sky. The Sabbath, gift of God, reaches out to embrace us. We halt what we are doing; we clear our brains of their hectic thoughts. Oh God! Purge our spirits of vexations and listen to the sacred silence echoing within. How cleansing is our breath, How inspiring is The Sabbath . Our souls fill with renewed wisdom and beauty. The Sabbath restores us.

86. THE SABBATH: WE SUSPEND DAILY ROUTINE

It is Sabbath. We suspend our daily devotion to routine We turn our thoughts to You God, Magnificent architect of the day of rest. From the very depths of our souls, we cherish, exalt, and revere You: Majestic sovereign of the cosmos.

87. THE SABBATH: LUSTROUS GEM IN TIME
THE SABBATH

Sabbath! Lustrous gem in Time! Your radiance brightens our lives, Your splendor burnishes our souls, Your purity crowns us with virtue. You transform us from our imperfect selves to the sterling people we hope to be.

88. THE SABBATH: TIME TO EXTOL THE WONDERS OF CREATION

For six days we quested with zeal to earn our daily bread and we failed to notice the wonders of the universe: the azure skies, the mighty mountains, the serene waters, the sparkling stars, the migrating birds or the thriving trees. Now it is Sabbath. We join hands with sisters and brothers throughout the world to honor these marvels and to rejoice in the wonders of Creation.

89. IN JOY WE GREET THE THE SABBATH

In joy we greet The Sabbath with joyous souls that glow like gold. We pray to You, Oh God, our cares to allay, so that we may Creation's glory behold. When we ponder the splendor of the world's formation, in an instant our souls are renewed, our hearts are filled with sublime elation, so that You will, once again Imbue our lives with beauty.

90. HOW SUBLIME IT IS TO GREET THE SABBATH

We thank You God for the sun that shines in the sky; we thank You for the world You Beautify. How sublime it is to greet The Sabbath. How inspiring it is to survey What You Created to bring solace and delight to every heart. How honored are we Your teachings to impart.

91. SABBATH IN WINTER

Wrinkled clouds whorl slowly beneath a purple mantled wintry sky. Sabbath is nigh spreading a dollop of joy to raise the spirits of a melancholy world.

92. EACH DAY IS GOD'S GIFT

Each day is God's gift to all, A blessed flower in the Garden of Eden filling our souls with holiness. But the Sabbath is a garland of Divine blossoms.

93. SABBATH GILDS OUR SOULS

The setting sun gilds the heavens as Sabbath approaches to gild our souls. How exquisite is this day— Glorious beyond words. Let's relish every flavor; let us every delicacy savor. This is the very moment we sanctify and magnify The Creator. Now is the moment we reach out to family far and wide. Let's salute The Sabbath Sovereign.

94. SABBATH: CLIMAX OF THE WEEK

This week crests towards its apogee and coalesces with eons of history. Ruby, emerald and coral plumes bejewel the evening sky, vestiges of the golden orb dazzle the eye. Heavenly harps strum and Celestial voices hum. All welcome The Sabbath Sovereign: hallowed presence, beauty pristine. All week long they have been stowing beacons of Divine Light glowing with God's gifts to humanity: decency, dignity, joy, harmony, healing, and charity. Now they leave their heavenly abode as the rhythm of life on Earth is slowed. Droplets of Divinity spread about and offer joy and healing to the world. Every soul is then reborn, which God's Glory will adorn. All human follies dissolve. To serve others we earnestly resolve. This day of rest all week for which we've pined, accords us much sought peace of mind. Sabbath is here to enfold each soul with God's Love, splendid to behold.

95. SABBATH IS REBORN AT DUSK

Dusk! The golden disk slips slowly beneath the horizon. Subtle strands of pastel swell the vast heavens. Sabbath is reborn bringing promise of joy, of health, and of peace. Sabbath is a buttress against the travail that will arise in the week to come.

96. THE CANOPY OF SKY IS BLUE

The canopy of sky is turquoise blue, the grass is emerald green, in between is every hue to enhance our souls serene. Sabbath is born 'mid song and prayer. It is a time holy and rare.

97. ACROSS THE GENERATIONS

From one generation to the next we read the sacred text to celebrate for all to see who we are and who we hope to be. The messages are very clear; their meanings we revere. We are all children of God: the rich, the poor, the sage, the clod. Every person of every race is crowned with God's Divine Grace. Every child, woman, and man has a place in God's holy plan. Let our passion for justice surge and let our inborn goodness emerge. Then our lives will be blessed and every Sabbath will be a day of rest, releasing ripples of goodness through out humanity.

98. COME WELCOME THE SABBATH

One and all! Come welcome The Sabbath Day. Every one! Open your hearts and pray as our ancestors taught us to do and as we teach our children, too. Every one! Raise your voices and sing. Every one! To goodness cling.

99. REBORN ON SABBATH DAY

Sabbath is reborn to adorn each soul. For this The Creator we extol. We are reborn to seek God's wise and loving ways. Words sublime spring up from within to sing praise to the Almighty, Author of Creation, Source of goodness, grace, nobility and salvation.

100. BEHOLD THE SABBATH SOVEREIGN APPROACHES

Behold The Sabbath Sovereign approaches; watch royalty drawing nigh, draped in regal splendor our lives to beautify. Draw closer Oh Sabbath Monarch, Gift of our exalted ancients. Make our souls gleam and glow and peace and joy within us will grow.

101. SILENT ARE THE HAWKERS

Silent are the hawkers who cawed their wares all week, Empty are the streets of shoppers who bargains would daily seek, The setting sun rims the clouds in glinting gold and crimson. The Sabbath Sovereign approaches our lives to beautify.

102. SABBATH STILLS THE WEEKLY CLAMOR

Oh Sabbath Day we pray that the weekly clamor is stilled. Cleanse the grime that like a fungus coats each soul. Let travail end and hope unfold. Release our worries and let joy reign. Uproot woe and gladness unchain.

103. SILENTLY SETS THE GOLDEN SUN

The moment before Sabbath unfolds, silently sets the golden sun across the hallowed horizon where it meets the Sea of Time. Work is stopped and burdens are made light. Our whispering souls invite God to rest with us today.

104. WELCOME! WELCOME! SABBATH SOURCE OF LIGHT

Welcome Sabbath, Fount of light, whose very essence illumines our lives ever so brightly, whose celestial radiance by God is Blessed. Release us from our daily plight. Guide us in our peaceful quest. Help us climb to heights sublime that renew our souls so bare. The Sabbath is Sovereign, a paradigm of lambent joy for all to share.

105. DAY TRUNDLES TOWARD THE NIGHT

Day trundles toward the night and Sabbath draws near. The golden rays of daylight will soon disappear. We'll find calm from life's demands severe and mantle ourselves in boundless hours of cheer. Oh Sabbath Sovereign! Our worries eschew. Oh Sabbath Monarch! Renew our zest. Sublime and grand thoughts will persevere and life's beauty we'll revere.

106. FROM SINAI'S MOUNT

From Sinai's mount we hear a call as Sabbath Day draws nigh. It is the voice that summons all pilgrims this day to sanctify. Gaze upon the setting sun behind the oaken tree, listen to the Angels chanting the ancient melody. Who is like Thee Oh God from which every creature springs? Who is like Thee Oh God that miracles daily brings? We stand upon the mountain peak and gates of Heaven open wide There we find The God we seek, our Comfort and our Guide. We free our lips and softly pray while soft clouds spin their fleece. In our souls it will always stay this sacred hour of peace.

107. ENDLESS IS SABBATH PEACE

The peace of Sabbath is endless; it flows and flows and flows. The bliss of Sabbath is peerless; it grows and grows and grows. The spirit of Sabbath is placid; it slows and slows and slows. The light of The Sabbath is ageless; it glows and glows and glows.

108. THE GOLDEN ORB OF THE SKY

The golden orb of the daytime sky drifts silently from view trailed by wisps of orange and pink unveiling a day our soul to renew. We welcome You, Oh Sabbath Monarch on the wings of a dove to turn the turmoil of daily life into a day of reflection and love. Oh sheltering majestic regent, show us the righteous road that we may the wisdom find that God upon us has bestowed. We will nestle beneath Your sheltering wing. Songs of praise to You we'll sing that will bring us peace of mind. Unfettered from doubt and anger will we that pathway find.

109. SABBATH SOVEREIGN: HERALD OF PEACE

Oh Sabbath Sovereign, Herald of Peace, fly into our souls, Drain Them of prodding anguish, fill them with serene joy.

110. THE WEEKLY QUEST FOR SABBATH.

Sabbath Time, apogee of the week, elevates God's Children out of their daily trough, ever higher toward a celestial crest. Throughout history have we, concretions of civilization, upheaval after upheaval, scintillating like sun bathed stones bonded together by the Holy Writ attain Sabbath peace. Sometimes fast, sometimes hastily, often deliberately. This scattered collection wanders the Sea of Time, Whose pelagic synchrony, at the pleasure of the merciful moon, undulates gracefully seeking out the next Sabbath when their souls will rise in whorls and eddy toward the sublime in every age and in every clime.

111. EARTH ENDS ITS DAILY ROUND

Sabbath approaches and the Earth finishes its daily run. We sit spellbound. No longer is there a frantic pace, No longer is the talk of the common place. Our home is quiet, mystically still. Sabbath has arrived and good will hovers. The world, with discord and in strife, is given new life.

Mother is dressed in her finest, with a tender smile blesses all in whispers warm and soft and sends her sagging spirits to cleansing zephyrs aloft. God, Source of our strength, she prays, help us embrace Your noble ways. She kisses each of us upon the forehead and the extra Sabbath Soul about us is spread. Father's eyes glisten as he rises to give thanks for family. We join in devout song that says it is to God we belong. Each of us adorns Sabbath and are reborn.

112. SIX DAYS EACH WEEK WE TOIL

Six days each week we toil with zest and on Sabbath we renew our quest to observe God all around and in every sight, in every sound: in every secret the seed discloses, in every melody the tune smith composes, in every canvas the artist paints, in every passion endured by saints, in every thought of the blessed sages, and in every battle the physician wages.

113. ON SABBATH WE PAUSE FROM DAILY ROUTINE

On Sabbath we pause from daily routine and marvel at the wonders of Creation. Warmly we welcome a day of rest with song and celebration and pledge homage to the Sabbath Monarch.

114. SABBATH: A DAY OF BEAUTY

Twilight appears and nears, a day without peers. At the behest of the Holy One, Earth bids au revoir to the Sun. The rough edges of the week are softened, burdens are lightened, The frenzied pounding of effort has slowed. The Sabbath Sovereign emerges from the Heavenly abode escorted by braided crimson cloud-piled plumes antique. Then we cast off workaday thought and the mystique of Sabbath raiment clad our lives with beauty, elegance, and joy. The Sabbath monarch, God's envoy, sows in our souls a sacred song for which each day we eagerly long. "How beautiful is this day," we extol, making this frail world sublimely whole.

115. BLESSINGS OF SABBATH BEAUTY

Blessed are we with Sabbath beauty spreading its splendor bright. Blessed are we with Sabbath peace that will reign throughout day and night. Blessed are we with Sabbath healing that makes an ailing body well. Blessed are we with Sabbath joy that all our ills expel.

116. BEACONS OF PEACE

Oh Sabbath lambency, beacons of peace, flickering arabesques of light, spread your weekly message of peace, grant God's Splendor to every soul. Oh God of all on this Sabbath we humbly pray, Send healing to restore the anguished, and untether our many mangled knots of woe. Direct our feet to walk straight paths and justice to everyone show. Inspire our minds, so that depths of wisdom we know.

117. MOTHER WHISPERS HER PRAYERS

Mother whispers her prayers beckoning God's splendor to illuminate our lives. The fading rays of the sun fill the room; candlelight flickers on our faces. Our fragile voices rise to sing, "Welcome angels. Enter. Bless you. Bring peace this Sabbath." Seraphim stirring in God's garden, attune to the heartfelt invitation lingering in their ears. They Gather about the golden flames and sing in chords sublime the ancient greeting from the Creator, "Peace unto you, this Sabbath Day." With outstretched wings they enrobe our souls; with calm they dance away.

118. BLESSINGS FROM AND TO MOTHER

Mother caresses her strand of pearls, worn by her mother before her, and her mother before her and countless mothers before them. Slowly she strikes a match, then lights the candle wicks. Flames sputter as her fingers circle the tapers like planets orbiting the sun. Then fingers soaked with tears of joy hide her eyes, glistening in the saffron flames whose spindly filaments of gold enclose undulating crescents of sapphire, as she whispers ancient blessings. Murmuring "Amen," she spreads her arms to bring her children close to her bosom sharing with them the second soul of Sabbath received from God, and which thrives within her. For one whole day her family, steadfast in its faith, cloaked in serenity, will bring doves of peace to every soul: God's gift.

119. A SABBATH PRAYER

May this Sabbath bring joy; may this Sabbath bring peace; may this SABBATH bring an end to woe, and may our myriads blessings grow.

120. NOT BY MYSTIC CHARIOT

Not by mystic chariot to heaven we ascend to God's sovereign throne. Nor rung by rung up Jacob's ladder we climb to reach God's splendor. But enfolded by Sabbath Angels, we rise and divine portals open. Amid the sound of trumpets, greeted are we in God's majestic sanctuary.

121. THANK YOU GOD FOR THIS WORLD

Thank You God for the world You Made where Tendrils of Grandeur Sprout and Braid. This SABBATH, a gift we bless, links us to You, the epitome of goodness through and through.

122. SACRED IS THE SABBATH NIGHT

In the sacred stillness of the Sabbath, night, watched from afar by stars sparkling bright, we hear the hymns the Angels sing and accept the peace they bestow. Our inner lights are all aglow. We add to Theirs our voices fluted, carried aloft by zephyrs muted. They return to us with God's Gift to share.

123. ANGELS ARISE TO SOW PEACE

Oh Sabbath, Angels we implore, that You bring a halt to every war. Untold are the orphans and widows, manifold are the wounded and maimed. In our souls sow seeds of lasting peace. God's Love in all we entreat release. Behold the gleam of the tapered Sabbath, lights! The dazzling sublime sights, bring joy and hope to every breast. That is the aim of our sacred quest.

124. BURNISHING THE LUSTER OF GRACE

Sabbath hospitality burnishes the luster of Grace; Sabbath, joy erases ignorance. Sabbath goodness embraces kindness. Sabbath, zest brings peace to every place.

125. THE CANDLES LIGHT OUR WAY

The sparkling Sabbath, lights illumine our steps through the dark paths of life. They chase despair away and dissolve every shred of strife.

126. ANCIENT FIRES TWINKLE IN THE SKY

Ancient fires twinkling in the sky greet the Sabbath Sovereign arriving from Its celestial abode, heralding a day of peace and mirth and release from travail. Oh Sabbath Sovereign may your mystique prevail throughout this coming week, healing the sick and making strong the weak.

127. ENFOLDS OUR SOULS

Wrapped around like a prayer shawl, the Sabbath soul embraces all. Serenity it brings and anguish it quells, awakening the hope that within us dwells. We'll turn the page of the week that passed with a prayer for peace. Infuse in us the will to be kind. Justice, justice we'll pursue and troves of compassion we'll accrue. There is much work yet to be done, but mending God's world has already begun. Let's resolve to feed needy and to absolve each thoughtless deed.

128. THE WAYS WE' VE BEEN BLESSED

As the sun slips silently in the West, we count the ways that we've been blessed. We recall the savory juices that bathed the tongue, and the sweet melodies that we heard sung. We recall the smiles upon children's faces,and the tenderness in our loved one's embraces. It is Sabbath, a moment to enchant, a time when love in our hearts to plant.

129. WELCOME, WELCOME SABBATH MONARCH

Oh soul of mine open wide your door, And welcome Sabbath Monarch once more, appearing from the astral domain to bring us peace and healing again. Greet the king with song; greet the king with dance; bask in celestial expanse.

130. REGARD THE LOOKING GLASS

Gaze into the looking glass. Behold a handsome lad, a comely lass. What the mirror to no one shows is a Sabbath soul whose patina glows, or a mind filled with wisdom's trove, or a heart beating with sincerest love.

131. EVERYBODY'S A RIPPLE IN GOD'S ETERNAL SEA

Everybody's a ripple in God's eternal sea. When my furrows ruffle you, yours make troughs in me. As you and I both ebb and flow in God's eternal sea we wrinkle other swirls, crinkling them unknowingly. They, in turn, crease other crests in God's eternal sea and shift their courses one degree and change their destiny. This is what Sabbath does. It changes us by one degree and to all others in God's eternal sea we immerse ourselves in peace and harmony.

132. SABBATH RESOLVES

'Though misunderstood let me understand others; though un-appreciated let me esteem others; 'though wounded let me heal others;'though oppressed let me cheer others;'though pained let me palliate others;'though anguished let me comfort others; 'though scorned let me forgive others. because we are all children of God.

133. SABBATH: GIFT OF HEAVEN

Oh Sabbath ! Blessed Gift of Heaven, a Diadem of Creation, Crowning each week with Glory, and radiating Peace, Healing, and Hope, inviting all to enfold themselves in the Gift.

134. DREAMING OF THE SABBATH MONARCH

In the twilight of this week, when the coming night seemed so bleak, I dreamed I saw The Sabbath Monarch Standing radiantly by my side to release my soul from my abysmal dread. Then God's blessing about me spread.

135. MERCIFUL ONE

Oh Merciful One, on this Sabbath Hear my prayer. Grant wisdom to all the peace seekers and bless all the peace makers.

136. BECOMING HOLY ON SABBATH

On this Sacred Sabbath day I pray that You help us find a way to heal the ailing, to feed the hungry, to house the homeless, to clothe the tattered, to soothe the battered, to raise the humbled, to comfort the mourner, to give joy to the downcast, to give hope to the forlorn; to give faith to the doubter and to grant wisdom to all.

137. A SABBATH PSALM

We start our toil on day one; on day six our work is done. The seventh day God Ordained for rest, a Sabbath: a day when all are Blessed. On this day we cast out care and unite as one in Sabbath prayer. In view of the flickering candle flames, o'er morsel of bread and drink we praise God's Name as our ancestors did in before. We thank You God for Your Creation. Again this eve we pledge to preserve and better Your World.

138. HOW BLESSED ARE WE

How blessed are we to watch the sun unfold each new day. How blessed are we that a baby's smile will our anguish melt away. How blessed are we to fill our brains with splendent rainbow hues. How blessed are we to perform deeds that a soul renews. How blessed are we to have the chance to beautify this world. How blessed are we to daily witness God's miracles unfurl.

139. MIRACLES ARE ALL AROUND

Miracles are all around. Look about and they are found in the sun that daily warms the earth, in the baby's cry at birth, in the genes of seeds we sow, in the sweet scents fragrant flowers bestow, in the thoughts sublime that fill the brain, in tinted rainbows after rain, in youthful yearnings of delight, in ancient stars that shine at night. Nothing is so sacred and pure as the elixir of Sabbath grandeur, which girds us with peace and rest for it is the time that God has Blessed.

140. THE SABBATH MEANS KINDNESS

Sabbath Day! You fill our souls with kindness, releasing us from woe, and for all an oasis, so that all Your Kindness will know. Your River of Divinity to us will ever flow.

141. ON SABBATH GLADNESS REIGNS

Banish sorrows, cast out pains, On Sabbath Day gladness reigns. Kindly Bless the ancestors, hallow the family, let our souls shine,. Oh God Divine.

142. SABBATH: SPLENDID AND MYSTIC

Sabbath Day, most honored of days, for you we scribe garlands of praise: sacred, hallowed, divine, clement, splendid, lambent, mystic, blessed, radiant.

143. SABBATH IS A SHELTER

Sabbath is a shelter where sorrows' pain is mended. Sabbath is a haven where a stranger is befriended. Sabbath is a refuge where torment's dread is quelled. Sabbath is a stronghold where loneliness is expelled. Sabbath is the eternal gift that unites us with what has been. Sabbath is the liberator that frees the good within. Sabbath is a day of joy that chants a sacred tune. Sabbath is a day of peace when we with God commune.

144. THE ROOTS OF WISDOM'S TREE

The roots of Wisdom's Tree generously feeds our souls with the fruit of God's Compassion. Looking back on this Sabbath we see how much our wisdom has grown. It is time to harvest Sabbath radiance within us glowing.

145. SACRED IS THE SABBATH EVE

Three Triolets of French Origin: abcadfeab

Sacred is the Sabbath eve
When candle light is all aglow,
And the blessings we humbly weave
Sacred is the Sabbath eve
When peace flows and worries leave,
And joys of soul like rivers flow.
Sacred is the Sabbath eve,
When candle light is all aglow.

146. OH SABBATH SOUL

Oh Sabbath soul fly into mine
And fill it with blissful calm,
And let your light within me shine,
Oh Sabbath soul fly into mine
And make me a holy shrine
And the blessings we humbly weave
Oh Sabbath soul fly into mine
And fill it with blissful calm,

147. HALLOWED IS THE SABBATH

Hallowed is the Sabbath Day,

Its splendor fills our spellbound souls

And disperses clouds of grey.

Hallowed is the Sabbath Day

When from the sun a beaming ray

Scintillates the sacred scrolls.

Hallowed is the Sabbath Day

Its splendor fills our spellbound souls.

148. SUFFERING CLINGS TO OUR SOULS

Daily suffering clings to our souls and sucks its marrow like a leech. On Sabbath we consecrate ourselves to what is worthy, which cleanses us of every evil deed, every ignoble thought, every selfish bent, and through every sacred song, every sublime dance, every psalm of thanksgiving, we ascend a sacred ladder to the Divine.

149. GATHERING AT MOUNT SINAI

It is Sabbath and we recount the story of Moses at Sinai's mount.

All generations wait for him to descend to share the sacred laws people must comprehend.

We, the mixed multitude, together pray that we will do as God Requires

And obey the laws of decency, and rise to the sublime heights each one aspires.

Again we will bond with You and You will be our God and

You will Teach us how to become a people unflawed.

150. HOLY IS THE SABBATH

How holy is Sabbath God Bathes it in Divine Light. How joyous is Sabbath when we with God unite. How holy is Sabbath! God fills its space with song, How joyous is Sabbath when we sing along. How holy is Sabbath God renews each weary soul. How joyous is Sabbath when we God supreme extol.

151. THANK YOU GOD FOR OUR BOONS

Oh God! We have so much to be thankful for: The food we eat, flowers sweet, our lacks so few, our friendships true. The right to learn, the chance to earn. No longer enslaved, from oppression saved. By You Redeemed, by loved ones esteemed. A home that is grand. Asylum in The Holy Land. Your warmth from above; Your Blessings of love. Amen

152. LISTEN TO THE VOICE THAT BECKONS

Listen to the voice that beckons to open our hearts to Sabbath peace. Hearken to the call to fill our souls with Sabbath grace. Now is the moment of profound devotion. Open wide the gates of innocence. Usher in the sweet, serene sounds of The Sabbath. Hear Them rippling in our ears like the wavelets in a tranquil sea. Watch them scintillating like diamonds in the setting sun. Hear! See! Dulcet voices of Angels from above fill our souls with serenity, and spread the abundance of God's sacred love. To one and all Sabbath is filled with quiet and calm. Sing with the Angels and give thanks for our trove of plenty.

153. FACETS OF THE SABBATH:
18 POEMS OF 18 SYLLABLES

a. Sanctify the Sabbath, diadem of the week, with friends, with kin, in joy.

b. On Sabbath Eve we strolled Eden's mystic woods and taste the fruit of bliss.

c. Sabbath joy exalts across clime, across time,. across creed, across class, across need.

d. The Sabbath Day draws nigh when the Spirit of God pervades every being.

e. The Sabbath Day forms an extra soul and we radiate serenity.

f. On the Sabbath we free ourselves of the mundane and unveil the sacred.

g. Sow the seeds of The Sabbath in all who search for peace and reap serenity.

h. Heirs to the sacred texts celebrate the Sabbath in scholarly study

i. Worship calms the soul yearning for Sabbath joy and frees mystic splendor.

j. The soul, Image of God, weary from the week's toil, finds rest on the Sabbath

k. Sabbath, island of peace 'mongst tossing swells of Time, welcomes all to its shores

l. Sabbath, wrapped in Grandeur, cloaks us in holiness to witness Creation.

m. Harps strum serene Sabbath songs before the holy ark and cheer the Divine.

n. A plaited wreathe of song enthrones The Sabbath to reign in every soul.

o. The Sabbath banishes despair through song and prayer and rebuilds shattered hopes.

p. Lambent Sabbath glows with saintly radiance of God's Eternal Fervor.

q. Sabbath enfolds our souls and we fly to Zion to hear the Levites sing.

r. Sanctify the Sabbath, the day God Rested then soar to the sacred.

154. LISTEN TO THE VOICE THAT BECKONS

Listen to the voice that beckons to open our hearts to Sabbath peace. Hearken to the call to fill our souls with Sabbath grace. Now is the moment of profound devotion. Open wide the gates of innocence. Usher in the sweet, serene sounds of The Sabbath. Hear Them rippling in our ears like the wavelets in a tranquil sea. Watch them scintillating like diamonds in the setting sun. Hear! See! Dulcet voices of Angels from above fill our souls with serenity, and spread the abundance of God's Sacred Love. To one and all Sabbath is filled with quiet and calm. Sing with the Angels and give thanks for our trove of plenty.

155. CELESTIAL CHOIR

Mellow Voices of The Celestial Choir melding in melodious, mystical runes rise in wisps and spiral aloft as we with God commune. Hear Their hymn. Oh Merciful One embrace us all with Your abiding love. Gaze upon the peaceful perch of the turtle dove.

156. SABBATH IS AN ISLAND

Sabbath is an island in an ageless sea. Distant from the roiling waves and enfolded by a heavenly canopy of countless glistening stars beckoning all to step into its cleansing waters and meet its majesty. Here and now, the stars announce, you are a haven for the oppressed, You are a refuge granting rest; You are a sanctuary where all are blessed by the compassionate God Sending healing to the distressed and granting joy to all who study the sacred law. Prayers, like tendrils, laden with delicately scented flowers, wrapped around God's Mercy transform us into the persons e aspire to be.

157. GOD REPAIRS BROKEN DREAMS

God, Mender of broken dreams and Renewer of shattered souls, Heal us on this Sabbath.

158. THE INFINITE GOD

Who but God Formed a mountain or Filled a sea, Or Painted a rainbow or Sculpted a tree? Who but God Taught the deer to leap and lambs to bleat and fish to swim or birds to tweet? But Can You God Purge our pain or oust our fears, or Quell our sorrows or dry our tears? No! You Gave us The Sabbath to purge pains, oust fears, quell sorrows, and dry tears. Open our lips in song and Make us strong.

159. GOD: TRUSTED FRIEND

Dear God, trusted friend, on this Sabbath day, Comfort the oppressed, Nurture the hungry, Free the enslaved, Heal the sick, Fashion the sublime. You who Arrange the orbits of the planets and Kindle the stars that ceil the night sky, Wrap us in the radiance of The Sabbath! Permeate us with Your Abundant Love, and we will transmit it to our loved ones as a heritage.

160. THE GOOD SOW KINDNESS

On this Sabbath Eve, God we pray, show the good how to sow kindness so that in this coming week we will reap holiness. On this Sabbath eve, show the upright how to plant piety, and in this week to come they will harvest Grace.

161. GOD: OUR REFUGE

God, our Refuge, Imbue us with the sacred and we will be holy. Infuse us with justice and we will be noble. Envelop us in Sabbath, and we will know peace.

162. SABBATH IS HERE

Sabbath is here. Embrace It. It quells woe amassed from toil that flogged us during the week that past. Welcome! Welcome! Sabbath Monarch. Inspire our souls with Your Love And bring us God's Blessings spread on the wings of a dove.

163. ON SABBATH WE QUENCH OUR THIRST

Each day of this past week our parched souls traversed desert. But on Sabbath we prayed to God, our Oasis, and quenched our thirst. Oh how You Fill our souls with such kindness that we will share and become a hallowed haven for all those in despair.

164. OASIS OF SABBATH

Parched in soul and whipped by swirling stresses of sorrow, we tramp through a desert throughout the week in search of calm. But on Sabbath, the storm abates. A sacred oasis of solace unfolds, We sip a cup of its serenity and become the true selves we seek to be.

165. BUDS OF PEACE SURROUND US

Buds of peace surround us every day of the week. On Sabbath, though, their beauty unfolds and unveils the exquisite peace we seek.

166. WELCOME, WELCOME SABBATH MONARCH

The sun dips slowly 'neath the horizon and olive wisps streak through the azure sky. Welcome, welcome Sabbath Sovereign, font of joy, Pouring forth Creation's blessings. Oh Sabbath Will Provide strength as we greet you. Sabbath arrives with a message of peace to nourish every yearning soul, and all of God's children far and wide gather to greet you. How truly Blessed are we to be children of God.

167. GOD OF COMPASSION FONT OF MERCY

God! On this Sabbath we humbly pray to You because You are Concerned for all peoples. We beseech You to Restore those in pain and to heal all those who ail. Through Your kindness they will find divine rest. Tenderly You Draw all in distress close to You where they find relief. Sincerely we all give thanks to You. Praised be Your Name. Hallelujah.

168. THANK YOU GOD FOR EVERYTHING

Thank You God for the morning sun and for the moon when day is done. Thank You God for the wind and rains that cleanse the earth on hills and plains. Thank You God for the blossoms of Spring. Thank You God for everything. Thank You God for the laws You provide, and for Your Teaching that is our guide. Thank You God for Your hand in love and for the gifts from heaven above. Thank You God for the peace that You bring. Thank You God for changing our angst to joy, our despair to hope, our baseness to beauty, our fears to courage, our flaws to blessings, and our distress to tranquility.

169. TO DO GOD'S WORK IS OUR DESTINY

God sculpted the mountains, filled the sea, Fashioned every insect and Planted every type of tree. God Spawned every species of fish, Propelled rivers to flow, Taught the birds to fly, Impelled the winds to blow. God Gave the animals freedom and bid the sun to shine, Painted prismatic rainbows and the planets to align. God Made creatures large and small and Made creatures of every kind that our minds enthrall. God Installed Time and Expanded Space, Then Magnified Creation with Mercy When all was completed as was designed, Sabbath, a time to rest, was then enshrined Sacred time, a time to guide our tongues to find words to comfort the bereaved, let our ears hear the anguish of the persecuted, and our endeavors protect them. Bless us with Your gifts of wisdom, mercy, and justice. Bless us with prudence, logic, and fairness.

170. RADIANT SABBATH

Radiant Sabbath, diadem of Creation, Burnish our souls. Light of the Divine Infuse our souls with healing on this day. Voices rise in song. Welcome, welcome SABBATH, day of joy.

171. SABBATH: A TIME OF BEAUTY

Sabbath unfolds like the petals of the rose unveiling beauty. Put away your anguish. Invite Celestial Envoys and bring peace to all.

172. SABBATH IS A TAPESTRY

Sabbath is a tapestry of fibers of every hue woven with devotion by each generation anew. Endless is the masterpiece of Mosaic born, and forever will our heritage our souls adorn.

173. SABBATH: SOURCE OF SERENITY

Upon us is Sabbath, source of serenity. A juncture in the chronicle of Time to rejoice with song and dance. A limitless venue of comfort in the geography of Space. It nourishes hope for the week to come. It is a respite when we reveal our true selves to The Creator as well as to our forbears in gratitude. It is a sweet moment, a peerless threshold to transcend from the routine to the Sacred. It shimmers with Divine Grace like a rare pearl glistening in the sun. It radiates God's Glory for all to enjoy.

174. SABBATH IS AN EDEN

SABBATH is an Eden away from the noisy crowds, where voices soft are heard of Angels beyond the clouds, and where the eyes behold daffodils gilding the sacred mound, where sweet attar of roses is in every whiff found. It is where ambrosia flavors every food that kindles every taste and where every thought the mind muses is wise, uplifting, and chaste. It is where each heart is beating with the rhythm of Creation and where every soul is set to worship God in adoration. At that moment our hands join with those who've gone before; at that moment generations to come will join with those of yore.; then every wounded soul will heal from Eden's curing balm, and will be made whole again.

175. BUDS OF PEACE SURROUND US

Buds of peace surround us every day of the week but on SABBATH their beauty swells and unveils the peace we seek.

176. ESSENCE OF SABBATH

Drink in the beauty of Sabbath, elixir of hope, with tenderness shines as an Eternal Light at the bosom of the living God. Let peace feed every cell of your being and fill you with warmth, with healing, and with joy.

177. DESCRIBING THE SABBATH

I search my mind for words to speak about The Sabbath, crown jewel of the week. It is a day of joy, a day of peace, a day of healing when all pains cease. A day to learn, a day to sing of the beauty that Angels Bring. So cloak yourself in Sabbath's delights. Your soul will soar to sublime heights. Share the peace you've just found with loved ones all around.

178. DAILY WE LONG FOR PEACE

Throughout this week we longed for solace and thirsted for peace. Now as Sabbath envelops us all burdens are lifted; all cares cease, and we see on the horizon the eternal stars shine upon our paths bringing us God's Blessings and guiding us to holiness.

179. GIVING THANKS ON THE SABBATH

Now is a moment of profound devotion. Open wide the gates of innocence. Admit the serene sounds of The Sabbath. Hear them rippling in your ears like the waves of a tranquil ocean, watch them sparkling like diamonds in the setting sun. Gentle voices of angels from above fill your souls with peace. Listen! Listen. Listen! Spread the abundance of God's Love. Thank God for your trove of plenty. Wrap yourself in their beauty. Breathe in God's Love deeply.

180. THE MOMENT OF CREATION

At the very moment of Creation, flutes in harmony played flourishing arpeggios, releasing every geometric shape of every size, saturated with the full spectrum of color, spinning and swirling in all manner of dance, celestial cells migrated and metamorphosed, and every finite species emerged out of the God imbued alleles pirouetting in sacred song. It was a moment of peace pervaded by resonant silence. Atoms of the Soul split and flowed into the amniotic lake of posterity where the sheen of the Divine Soul forever bathes every cell with Grace. Then Sabbath was born and crowned Creation.

181. SABBATH LIGHT SURROUNDS US

Sabbath lights surround us and purify our souls. It soothes our sorrows and douses flames of hatred. It strips away petty jealousies and bathes us in waters of forgiveness. Serenely, it wraps us in holiness and brings us close to God.

182. SABBATH: CANOPY OF TRANQUILITY

The tired ribs of each lusterless day of work vault and arc toward the azure skies. It bore a canopy of tranquility from which emerges radiant Sabbath— Soft, light, serene. A day of rest. A day of peace.

183. SABBATH BEDECKS US IN HOLINESS

Sabbath bedecked in holiness pervades my humble soul, and I, a mere jot in time, the eternal God Extol for the beauty of Creation, a divine gift that grows in every moment, and does The Sublime enshrine.

184. SABBATH: PORTAL TO PEACE

Oh Sabbath! You are a terminal to clamor and a portal to peace.

185. SABBATH RESOLVE

Before the family and friends gathered here on this Sabbath we solemnly dedicate ourselves to make this world better for others: sisters and brothers of every inclination of every nation, of every station, vow to honor God's Creation.

186. FROM DAILY TURMOIL WE SEEK RELEASE

From daily turmoil we seek release, then wrap ourselves in Sabbath peace. Avidly we thirst for a day of rest, and to be by God Divinely Blessed.

187. SABBATH: ANOTHER PERSPECTIVE

It was the very first Sabbath since Creation, the moment God Ordained a day of rest. A bright light slowly emerged from the firmament. That Divine flicker has scintillated since the dawn of Time, to kindle the Sabbath, God's Gift to every race and every nation.

188. WE MEET OUR FORBEARS ON SABBATH

On Sabbath we meet our forebears at the hem of Time, and sing a new song praising The Creator Whose Essence Shines with delight and beams to us in rays of peace. How grateful are we to those who have gone before us and mantled us with warmth and wisdom. Daily we seek their sparkling judgment to share their noble purity with posterity.

189. ON THE SABBATH HEAVEN'S CROWN SETTLES ON US

We wrap ourselves in prayer shawls and meditate upon God's grand scheme. Then a Heavenly crown settles upon us and we hear the sweet music of The angels. Then we behold the glories of Creation. Our souls are restored, our minds grow wise, and our bodies heal.

190. ON THE SABBATH THE SUN RADIATES WARMTH

During our weekly odyssey in quest of serenity storms brew, clouds scud, waves crash. As we approach Sabbath day, the storms abate, the clouds clear, the sun radiates warmth. Behold on the horizon is The Sabbath a sanctuary, resplendent with golden daffodils and releasing the scent of attar of roses. Glorious healing calm infuse our souls.

191. ON THE SABBATH TIME SLOWS

Today is Sabbath. Time slows, we savor its silence, we treasure its beauty, we embrace its healing, we cherish its gift.

192. SABBATH ENTREATS CLING TO THE SACRED CREED

The dulcet voice of Sabbath beseeches all without regard to gender, race, or nation to adhere to the sacred creed inscribed in The Scriptures that exults the Author of Creation. They will find healing, wisdom, peace, joy, and redemption.

193. WORLDWIDE FAMILIES WELCOME SABBATH

Sisters and brothers fathers and mothers from every direction: North, South, East, West. At God's Behest join hands and welcome Sabbath in song. Invite the world, we entreat, to sing along praising God, Fount of perfection. for providing us with a spell for reflection.

194. ON SABBATH GOD ATTIRES US IN DIVINITY

It is Sabbath, a blink in time for us to dwell in eternity When God clads us in divinity, angels enrobe us in majesty, Sages crown us with wisdom, and saints embrace us with empathy. They beseech us to be their partners in enhancing this world with divinity, majesty, wisdom, and empathy in enhancing this world with divinity, majesty, wisdom, and empathy.

195. WE FIND PEACE ON SABBATH

Sabbath is a time when our labors cease. Sabbath is a place, a sanctuary where we find peace. Sabbath is a mood that spreads joy throughout the soul. Sabbath is a healer that makes the splintered self whole.

196. ON SABBATH WE ARE FILLED WITH DIVINITY

Dear caring and heedful God, too often I feel empty, hollow, useless, aching. But on The Sabbath You Fill my being with divinity, joy, goodness, and peace. Because of You I suffer less; because of You I heal; because of You, I despair not, but hope. Because of You I agonize not, but am at ease. How grateful am I to You Dear caring and heedful God!

197. ON THIS SABBATH GUIDE US HOW TO LIVE WITH HOPE

On this Sabbath, dear caring and heedful God, Show me how to control my passions and become strong, patient, and filled with confidence. I can rise above my failures, I can find the courage to better myself, I can, as Your partner, improve the World. With utmost sincerity, I pray You unclog the love that lies dormant within my soul.

198. O GOD HELP US FIND DIVINE JOY

We look around us, there is so much we do not fathom: misfortune, rage, illness, calamity. Dear caring and heedful God, on this Sabbath help us find the joy that flows through our souls. Help us sanctify ourselves, so that we can reap the words You have sown, and bless Your Creation.

199. O GOD CREATOR OF SABBATH

Through the gloaming Sabbath appears at dusk, I look inward and unveil to You every thought that is in my heart, every feeling that is in my soul: my joy, my sorrow, my fears, my hopes. Oh God, Shepherd of the lonely, the ailing, and the oppressed, You are our friend, our healer, and our font of cheer. How truly blessed are we to live according to Your sacred text at Your behest. The Sabbath that You Created melts our trials and nurtures our strengths.

200. JOINING MY PEOPLE ON SABBATH

Each Sabbath when I arise, I open my eyes and scan the skies. The mysteries of Creation are awesome to behold. Before my very eyes I watch unfold the path from the ordinary to the holy. I begin my trek up to heights unknown. When I reach the peak, too frightened am I to speak. I open my mind and take in human history wrapped in joy, pain, and mystery. For a moment my senses are numb. There am I in the midst of Sabbath's holy day, engulfed in prayer to You, God, and express a sincere blessing that I, with human history am coalescing.

201. A PRAYER FOR SABBATH

Sing a new song unto God. Sing it loud; sing it clear. Awake, awake! Sense God's Radiant Glory. Thank You God for the treasures bestowed upon us. I vow to dispel despair, and to soothe the ailing. I pledge to stamp out sadness and to usher in joy. I vow to eliminate darkness and to beam Your Light to every soul. On this Sabbath I promise to devote my life to make this, Your World, better.

202. FACETS OF SABBATH

Sabbath envelops us in serenity. Sabbath sheathes us in healing. Sabbath cloaks us in divinity. Sabbath enfolds us in joy. Sabbath engulfs us in beauty. Sabbath surrounds us in radiant light. Sabbath, the week's crown jewel, is a cocoon out of which we are reborn to nobility.

203. JOIN THE ANGELS IN A SABBATH HYMN

Sabbath is inching closer. The sun slips below the horizon. Hearken to the plucking of the strings of the ancient lyre. Give an ear to the strumming of the harp of yore. In the distance a choir of angels raise their vibrant voices and sing, "Oh God! How magnificent is Your Blessed Creation." At that very tick of time voices throughout the world join and exalt God in a new song with gladness.

204. SABBATH: CREATION OF GOD

Sabbath, a hiatus during the week, a time to reflect on the wonders God Performed, We pause to meditate on the miracles God Wrought. Who but God Invented Sabbath, a day of rest, a celebration of joy, a time of healing? Who but God Designed Sabbath, a spell to renew our bodies and minds? When our ancestors witnessed God's awesome power, they crowned the majestic Almighty "Monarch of the universe." On Sabbath we stop to exalt the Cosmos. On Sabbath we extol the Origin of Creation.

205. SABBATH: GOD'S GIFT

God Gave the world The Sabbath Day as a day of rest, and remember and marvel at Creation. The Sabbath is a day God Blessed, a day to attain with deep-rooted ardor Heaven's salvation.

206. SABBATH: LINKS US TO GOD

Generations of old hallowed The Sabbath, as will generations yet to come. The Sabbath renews the body, and revives the soul. The Sabbath restores our courage, It breathes new life in our sagging spirits. Ours is an everlasting covenant with God. We are blended with God, our Friend and Partner.

207. ON SABBATH WE FIND THE WISDOM OF MOSES

This morning we searched our soul and found it was empty. Now as The Sabbath grows near lights shines from the sacred words of the Elders and it liberates from within us dormant wisdom, caring, joy, and serenity.

208. GOD MAKES SABBATH SACRED

On the sixth day of Creation, God's Essence filled every soul with Divine droplets to be passed on unaltered from one generation to the next. On that first Sabbath, tenderly each soul was burnished with nobility. Compassionately, each was gilded with kindness. At a mystic moment, God Permeated each soul with grandeur, and infused each soul with splendor. Then, was The Sabbath sanctified a day of rest, joy, and healing. Then was The Sabbath consecrated a Holy Day.

209. SABBATH RENEWS US

Sabbath transforms us from the ordinary to the sacred. On that day we stroll through the Garden of Eden and are dazzled by the fragrant scent of lavender, lilies, and lilacs. We are moved by the dainty shapes and hues of asters, azaleas, and anemones. There, in the middle of the Garden, a new soul is added to the mundane we are, a soul that apprehends all aspects of the Divine Creation, a soul that is Sabbath blessed, a soul imbued with health, vigor and zest, a soul that vouchsafes our destiny.

210. OH THAT THIS SABBATH WILL BE FILLED WITH PEACE

May this Sabbath be filled to overflowing with peace, mutual respect, and healing that restores every fiber of our beings; for this we thank and extol the everlasting majestic God, Guardian of our souls blessed with solace.

211. THE SABBATH: RESTORER

We pray on the Sabbath that You Oh God Spread about us Your Divine Presence that will renew us with vigor. We entreat that You Infuse our hollow souls with holiness, Restore our defeated spirits with serenity, Knead our broken hearts with kindness, and buttress our weak wills with resolve. God! Teach us how to forgive. Teach us to absolve those who harm us through malice and willful intent or through mortal artlessness. Above all help us to acquit ourselves of our own misguided efforts.

212. WELCOME TO THE SACRED SABBATH

Earth journeys across the horizon bidding good-bye to the sun whose rays gleam through a lapis shawl erupting in fuchsia streaks in the evening sky. Now on the cusp of the sacred, we focus on Time to welcome the Holy Sabbath when grief dissolves, anguish ceases, and anger abates. On The Sabbath peace emerges from its celestial sanctuary and envelops and transforms us to the persons we aspire to be. How excellent and noble it is to know Sabbath Peace. On this Sabbath Day may our splendor increase.

213. SABBATH : TIME AND PLACE

Everyone has a time and place that beckons to them, where serenity reigns and problems fade. The soul is that place and The Sabbath is that time. Then and there shortcomings are ignored, errors are forgiven, and virtues, lauded. Then and there we meet The Sacred. Come let's welcome The Holy Sabbath, elixir to parched spirits.

214. THE ARRIVAL OF THE SABBATH

As the scintillating sun sets slowly in the west, we renew our weekly quest to be free of daily routine.Then with an open heart we welcome the Sabbath monarch. Deep within our souls our forebears still thrive. In our memory their feats still survive. In the epicenter of the Sabbath soul is God, compassionate God, merciful God, Whose majesty in our prayers we fervently laud. Sabbath is here for all to enjoy every man, every woman, every girl, and every boy.

215. MUSIC IN THE HEAVENS ANNOUNCE THE SABBATH

The sun is shrinking in the western sky; a time to bid the week that passed good bye. It is The Sabbath and in the Heavens angels strum on their lyres, Cherubs hum in their choirs to announce to the world that Sabbath is near. A time to celebrate in joy, peace, healing, and good cheer.

216. SABBATH AT SINAI'S CREST

Trekking to the crest of the week We pilgrims reach the Sabbath, the holiest of days. We gather at Sinai's crest to behold myriads of forebears embracing the sacred scrolls and singing serene, sacred hymns. How regal yet humble is this day of rest, our weekly quest, Crowned by God, and eternally Blessed.

217. JOINING SOULS ON THE FIRST SABBATH

Late on the sixth day of Creation a Divine essence sprang from God's soul. Sacred, majestic specks burnished with holiness amalgamated with the souls of the human family, Blessing them, consecrating them, sanctifying, and gilding them for all time with mercy and justice.

218. MYRIAD OF BLESSINGS SPIRAL TO GOD

It is Sabbath eve and myriads of blessings spiral to God, in thanks that the week of toil has ended, and that God's Grace has extended to a flock of the grateful, who laud every miracle they beheld in the week that passed, unsurpassed beyond anything they had asked.

219. ANSWER TO OUR PRAYERS

This past week a dark cloud hovered over us. We prayed passionately for the sun to come out. Then on The Sabbath God Answered our prayers. The sun shone in the world throughout.

220. IMPLANT IN US DIVINE COMPASSION

On this Sabbath implant in us Seeds of Divine Compassion. Make us sensitive to the needs of others. Help us feel the anguish of the oppressed. Days of the down-trodden are darkened by their wretchedness. Your Light, Oh God, opens the portals to beauty. Help us bring joy to the world, and we'll plant Sabbath Rest in their souls.

221. SURROUND US WITH YOUR GLORY

On this Sabbath Oh God, surround us with Your glory, Endow us with Your wisdom, Open our eyes, Oh God, to the beauties of Nature. Open our hearts to the oppressed, Open or minds to the mysteries of the universe, Open our souls to the helpless. Then Sabbath will raise us to the sublime. Then Sabbath will open the Gates to the Sacred.

222. SABBATH: ENDOWED BY GOD

Our forebears hallowed Sabbath, Endowed by God, reviving their spirits, restoring their minds and renewing their bodies. They conferred upon all future generations their sacred trust to honor the holy day through prayer, song, and kind deeds, bequeathing to all future generations a sacred legacy to enrich God's gift of Sabbath rest.

223. PRAYER ELIXIR OF THE SOUL

On our journeys from last Sabbath to this Sabbath, we prayed ardently for God's guidance. Prayer, elixir of the soul, essence of humility, permeated our beings, and made our fragmented selves whole again. Today we are closer to God. Today we are no longer flawed.

224. AWED BY GOD'S MARVELS

It is Sabbath and we are awed by the wonders God Has Wrought. When we gaze at them we clearly behold the artistry of each flower: the whorls, the scrolls, the painted petals, the fragrant aroma. We also fathom the goodness in humanity, which radiates from God's Mercy. Amazed are we by the snow-capped timeworn mountains, and the frothy rolling cerulean sea. How comforting are the gentle zephyrs cooling the skin on a hot day. How steady is the solar disc by day and the ancient splinters of lights twinkling during the Stygian night. What Divine wisdom Created our wonderful, awesome world? We tremble with joy at what God Unfurled.

225. ON SABBATH WE PRAY FOR WORLD PEACE

This Sabbath I pray that You, God, Knit together every living soul and bring harmony into Your world. Teach all to care for one another: every sister and every brother of every race from every place. Teach them to deplore hatred and war, and with all of the world's families to find rapport.

226. SABBATH: CENTER OF MY SOUL

Sabbath is the very center of my soul. Pervaded it is with kindness that radiates to every fiber of my being, From there to every soul encircling me. How truly blessed am I with Sabbath peace and joy, a gift to share with my peoples.

227. SHINE YOUR LIGHT ON US

God of compassion and justice, on this Sabbath Shine Your lustrous light upon Your World. Much of it is beautiful, healthy, and wise, but some parts of it need to be revised. Please Guide us in a path to mend broken hearts, and become a friend to each whose souls in darkness dwell, who must find ways to excel. Then we, pauper and prince, will not only survive, but will thrive.

228. A SABBATH PLEA TO GOD

On this Sabbath, dear God, Creator of the cosmos, Mender of our shattered hopes and nurturer of our aspiring dreams, Help us find the sacred in the ordinary and the beauty in the lackluster. Teach us how to discover the miracles You Wrought and how to create new ones. Teach us to build and not destroy. Help us foster a more compassionate world through kindness and charity.

229. RESTORED ON THE SABBATH

Like their ancestors before them and alive within them, they consecrate themselves to God and dedicate themselves to noble endeavors. On Sabbath they are refreshed, restored, revitalized, and are Divinely Blessed. Rested, they thank God for the past week and pray for strength to manage the week to come.

230. SABBATH AROUND THE WORLD

Sabbath is drawing near around the world, in Rome and Nome, in Pretoria and Astoria, in Oslo and Moscow, in Paris and Dallas, in York and Cork, in Savannah and Havana, in Budapest and Bucharest. Sabbath arrives North, South, East, and West. On that day we reach the crest of Sinai's majestic peak, too awed to speak. We look about and see that everywhere in the world it is The Sabbath.

231. SABBATH MINISTERS OF PEACE

During this past week I was arranged of pieces, particles, splintered slivers. Now it is Sabbath and ministering Angels, Heralds of God, Have Assembled to greet me, mend me, and make me whole. Welcome Couriers of God. Come close to me and Bless me with peace. As You leave I exalt and revere You. O venerated Ones, how truly blessed am I.

232. SABBATH: ANCHOR OF OUR SOULS

Sabbath You anchor our souls, be the seas roiling or calm. Sabbath! You offer balm to the despairing, and provide solace to the caring. Sabbath! You unmoor us from pangs of doubt, and grant rest to the devout. Sabbath! Wrap us in your serenity and infuse us with Your Divinity.

233. GOD ETERNAL

God, Eternal. Friend and Guide Dwell within us and there reside. Calm as oceans deep and blue, Strong as mountains tall and true. Enfold us in Your warm embrace. Protect us in Your sacred space. Make us wise so we may know the path of light for us to go. This Sabbath Day we keenly pray to pledge our lives e'er to portray Your ways so true and ideal as well. In Your Kindness we'll always dwell. From dawn of days a laurel You Wore. Divine monarch It is You we adore. You have been, are and e'er will be the crown of Grace, Soul's majesty.

234. THE SABBATH DAY: ZENITH OF THE WEEK

My parents, like those who preceded them, opened my eyes to the radiance which the Sabbath Day beam.These are their legacy which I pass on. The Sabbath is the crown of Creation.

235.IMMERSE YOURSELF IN SHABBAT

Hours before the onset of The Sabbath we embroider with golden threads the canvas of Time. Peace interlaces with Joy, Weft of God, and cloaks us in Heavenly Grace.Wearing the cloak of The Sabbath gladdens us throughout the week

236. IMMERSE YOURSELF IN THE SABBATH

On The Sabbath we screen out sorrows and cares of the past week and behold the wonders of Creation, God's Gift to every race and every nation. On Sabbath we sieve the sorrows and cares and raise the curtain to behold the wonders of Creation.

237. THE SABBATH, SEED OF SERENITY

Upon us is The Sabbath, Seed of Serenity, Fashioned in Heaven by Angels Divine. Nurtured by God sown in our souls by God's Envoy for us to enshrine. It flowers God's Glory for all to enjoy.

238.AWAKE1 AWAKE1 IT IS THE SABBATH

Slumber no longer. Awake! Awake! We open our souls to God's Mercy, Greet God's Glory with song, And listen to the angels who sing along.We remove ourselves from the daily routine and bask in Sabbath Sheen.

239.THE BOND BETWEEN GOD AND THE PEOPLE

After the Heavens and earth were set in motion and planets spun at their own rhythm plants and animals flourished. God Blessed The Sabbath Day to Honor Creation forging the bond between the Divine and peoples of every nation.

240. IT IS THE GLORIOUS SABBATH

The Glory of God Scintillates throughout the cosmos and Enters our souls, Transforming us into the persons we aspire to be: Merciful, Patient, Considerate, Appreciative, Cherished, Admired, Restored. Thank You God for the Gift of Light.

241. ON SABBATH WE WITNESS THE BEAUTY OF CREATION

It is the Sabbath. Silence reigns. Then through the hush quiet we talk to God and we listen to the distant voice of God Whispering through eons of history. Our souls awaken and we cast out our worries. Then we witness the Beauty of Creation.

242. MAJESTY OF THE SABBATH

How Majestic is this Sabbath Day; it Crowns Time in Glory. It Reigns supreme among all days. It Awakens the goodness in our hearts; Whets our minds; and Enriches our souls.We join hands with our peoples of the past, of the present, and of the future to praise God, Author of the universe, with gratitude through prayer, through song, and through dance.

243. THE SABBATH EXPUNGES TRAVAIL

The Sabbath Expunges travail from our souls; It Edits our shortcomings; It Rescinds our flaws; It Expands our talents; It Boosts our qualities; and It Praises our achievements;

245. BEGINNING OUR MOUNTAIN CLIMB

As each new day begins climb the unbeaten rough and rugged path up the mount that leads to God. Scaling the rocky crags, we look toward the mountain crest glistening in the sun, harbinger of hope. Upward! Upward! We climb higher with the firmest resolve to reach the tor. Each step clears the debris cluttering our minds and littering our souls. We stop and reflect on what life is: stormy, arduous, joyful and also calm and promising. Then a shawl of peace enwraps us, and we sow serenity and reap reason. It is The Sabbath, Island of tranquility. Angels Guide us in our descent down the smooth path that we paved in our ascent. We marvel at the Grandeur of Creation. At this moment the world is better because of our humane heart and decent deeds.

246. PARTNERS WITH GOD

We have been partners with God during the week gone by. Together we sowed seeds of love and defy the world gone awry. At this moment The Sabbath is growing nigh and the time has arrived for us to rest and reap the rewards of a better world that we with God have devoutly blessed.

247. THE SABBATH: A PRICELESS GIFT

The Sabbath is a seed that we sow in our hearts to open our souls to the grandeur of Creation. It sweetens our dreams and fills us with hope that tomorrow will be even better than today. Oh what a priceless gift is The Sabbath.

248. EXALTED IS THE SABBATH DAY

How exalted is this Sabbath day, an instant in history, crowning Creation with Glory and dispersing serenity throughout the cosmos.

249. ON THE SABBATH WE CHERISH ITS GRANDEUR

On the Sabbath we cherish its grandeur. We regard its Splendor; we burnish its Luster and sow love in our hearts. Nourishing and honoring God's Creatures of yesterday, today, and tomorrow.

250. PARTICLES ARE WE IN THE COSMOS

Although we are but specks in the expanse of Space and mere trifles in the annals of Time yet we build upon our heritage and enrich God's Cosmos.

251. MOSES LEGACY TO PROSPERITY

Moses bequeathed his legacy to posterity. Remember and heed The Sabbath and keep it holy: Not to the Children of Israel solely but to all peoples to observe a day of rest with sincerity and conviction: their souls to renew and with holiness imbue.

252. SABBATH PEACE STILLS OUR ANGUISH

Sabbath peace enfolds us. It stills our anguish and calms our souls. It mends our ways; restores our resolve; and rebuilds our lives. How refreshed are we reciting Sabbath psalms; how revived are we singing Sabbath songs.

253. CHILDREN OF ALL RACES CELEBRATE THE SABBATH

In hushed stillness as The Sabbath nears before the Angels Sang their hallowed hymns, Cuppe´d hands masking our eyes we hearken to the hopeful voices of the Children of all races throughout eons of Time. Celebrating the splendor of this holy day by thanking God for this day of rest and for the Blessed Legacy Bestowed upon us.

254. SABBATH PRAYERS RESOUND IN OUR EARS

Sabbath prayers resound in our ears as it has done for thousands of years: praising the Merciful with devout devotion; extolling Creation with joyous emotion. We pause at this Sacred Threshold to laud The Magnificence of Almighty God.

255. THE WAYS WE HAVE BEEB BLESSED THIS WEEK

Let's count the ways we have been blessed this past week: we heard the sweet sounds of the birds in the early morning; we felt the breeze wafting in the trees; we smelled the sweet fragrance of flowers; we prayed that the wounds of the sick will heal; we softened the sorrows of the mourner; we helped the needy; we received the crown of peace. Sabbath, a gift to all, for all these we extol God.

256. SABBATH, THE CORE OF THE UNIVERSE

At the core of the soul of the universe is The Sabbath, Herald of peace, Envoy of God's Glory.

257. CLOSED IS THE CURTAIN ON THE WEEK THAT PASSED

The curtain closes on this past week's toil. The Sabbath prepares us for the week ahead filled with hope and free of dread.

258. THE SABBATH AN OASIS OF SERENITY

This past week we wandered in a desert, sometimes without aim; sometimes with purpose. Now it is The Sabbath an oasis of serenity, engulfing our souls with Divine Radiance and sowing peace, hope, and calm in the terrain of our lives.

259. USHER IN THE SABBATH TOGETHER

Let's usher in the Sabbath together. Let's lift our spirits so strong; let's raise our voices in song and pray for all in God's World to get along. Then the peace of Sabbath will dwell within us all week long.

260. ON SABBATH THE GATES OF HEAVEN OPEN

It is The Sabbath. The Gates of Heaven open wide. Heavenly Angels Welcome all. They Guide all pilgrims seeking serenity on to the Paths of peace and joyous pleasure.

261. THE SABBATH ARRIVES WITH WISDOM, SMILES, AND GLADNESS

The Sabbath is arriving bringing wisdom to our minds, smiles to our souls, and gladness to our hearts.

262. WE CELEBRATE THE GLORY OF CREATION

It is The Sabbath, a holy day, summit of the week when yesterday joins tomorrow, To sanctify today. At this moment of sacred Time we celebrate the glory of Creation with prayer, with song, with dance, with art and with kind feelings toward all of life.

263. REVIEW OF THIS PAST WEEK

When we review the events of the past week what stands out is the Beauty of Creation: how the tint of the birds color our lives; how the sounds of our animal friends gratify our ears; how the fragrance of the flowers cleanse our noses; how we savor the tastes on our tongues. It is The Sabbath -a time of rest filled with moments to reflect on all of God's Gifts.

264. SABBATH: A TIME TO MEDITATE

It is The Sabbath: A time to meditate on the Glory of Creation. The day is filled with the promise of renewal, the restoring of our souls, and the rejuvenating of our bodies.

265. WELCOME SABBATH: A DAY OF REST

Welcome Sabbath, a day of rest. Fill our beings with holiness. Sharpen our judgment, fortify our regard for friends and family, bringing cheer to the ailing and comfort to the grieving. For all of these we bless and give thanks to God.

266. LISTEN TO ANGELS BECKONING US TO WELCOME THE SABBATH

Listen to Angels beckoning us to welcome the Sabbath with hymns. For one entire day each week they inhabit our souls and rejoicing with sacred song make us holy.

267. PARTNERS ARE WE WITH GOD

Partners of the one and only God That Formed the Cosmos and all the treasures that are ours to behold. Bless Creation with sincere thanks! Let us with rest on the Sabbath and with God
Embrace its holiness.

268. THE MANTLE OF PEACE IS COMPLETED

Each weekday God's Angels weave silver strands of serenity on a sacred loom. On The Sabbath the mantle of peace is completed for all to don for the holy day.

269.THE SABBATH A DAY OF REST GOD HAS BLESSED

The Sabbath, when peace and healing coalesce- a time from all travail to divest. The Sabbath, a day of rest: a sacred day that God Has Blessed.

270. THE SABBATH MONARCH ENVELOPS US IN GLADNESS

Unfolding the curtain of The Sabbath we rise to greet the Sabbath Monarch who envelops us in gladness, peace, and healing. At that moment we dedicate ourselves to a sacred purpose of bringing gladness, peace, and healing to all.

271. OH GOD! ON THE SABBATH WE ARE RENEWED

All week long have we toiled to enrich this world. You, God, Graciously Gave us the strength to bear our loads. For this we give You thanks. On The Sabbath You Endow us with courage to endure our struggles. Renewed, we sincerely give You thanks.

272. TRUMPETS AND LYRES HERALD THE ARRIVAL OF THE SABBATH

Trumpets and lyres herald the arrival of The Sabbath, the ordained day of rest; vaulted heavens echo their call. Beckoned are we to ascend to the heights of peace and healing sublime. With joy we hearken to the knells of the celestial bells. Arising we greet the Sabbath monarch. With outstretched arms we embrace each.

273. ANGELS BURNISH OUR SOULS

The Sabbath nears. Angels from Heaven Appear to burnish souls weary from toil and turmoil. Hearken to their sweet voices as they hallow this day with song. They will attend you from this day to the next. In their wake they will transmit an aura of peace issuing from healing, and joy.

274. GOD ETERNAL FRIEND AND GUIDE

God Eternal, Friend and Guide, Dwell within us sanctified. On Sabbath Make us holy to do good deeds and to honor Your serene Monarchy. Reign forever and sow contentment in every being. Open our hearts to its melody; Unbolt your soul to its harmony. Hear the Angels Sing an anthem to God's Creation, coaxing the Holy Spirit to ascend to the most Exalted Eminence of Divinity.

275. O SABBATH YOU FREE US TO LIVE A GOOD LIFE

Oh Sabbath! You Anchor our souls, be the seas roiling or calm.

Oh Sabbath! You Offer balm to the despairing and Provide solace to the caring.

Oh Sabbath! You Unmoor us from pangs of doubt Granting rest to the devout.

Oh Sabbath! Wrap us in Your serenity and Infuse us with Your Divinity.

276. DAILY WE SEARCH FOR THE HOPEFUL

Daily we trudge through tangled thickets of memories to winnow the forlorn from the hopeful. We search for a healthy, promising "stalk" plant it, and watch it grow. As it flowers we delight in its splendor. When it matures we open its hull and disperse seeds of benevolence.

277. ON THE SABBATH I SOAR LIKE AN EAGLE

On The Sabbath I am lifted by Your love like an eagle soaring on a current of air, dipping, and floating on azure clouds. I am carried into your Heart and Soul where I will dwell forever.

278. THE SABBATH MONARCH ADORNED IN SERENITY

God Anointed The Sabbath Monarch, adorned in serenity, to reign forever and sow contentment in every being. Listen with your heart and soul. Hear the Angels Sing an anthem to God's Creation. They coax the Holy Spirit to ascend to the most Exalted Eminence of Divinity. Let us join God's Messengers in song; dance with Them; spread Their joy.

279. OH SABBATH YOU ARE SO MUCH TO ME

Oh Sabbath! You're a flower scrolled and scented. You're its hue brightly pigmented; You're the nectar sweet and tender; You're the blossoms in their splendor. You're the music tinged in gold; You're the lyrics I unfold; You're its rhythm in my heart; You're its rhymes so sweet yet tart. You embody the sacred shrine where all about is God Divine.

280. MONARCH SABBATH YOU CROWN OUR WEEK.

Oh monarch Sabbath You crown the week with beauty and with grace and surrounds us with the love of God. Oh monarch Sabbath how our souls embrace you. A rainbow you sow to cloak our souls and echoes Divine wisdom in Holy scrolls. You are always in our thoughts. Our hearts pulse in a joyous cadence from the pleasure you give us. How truly blessed are we.

281. THE HEALING BLESSING FROM THE SABBATH MONARCH

When the strands of my life unlace and my fractured soul goes awry

My eyes drop a tear. Yet I persevere.

I search for a solution to end my persecution.

Then from Heaven comes the clarion call arise and greet the Sabbath Monarch

Who lovingly Embaces me and reverently Blesses me with Divinity.

282. SABBATH SPIRALS IN THE SEA OF TIME

Swirling swells of serenity spiral in the Sea of Time, cloaking our beings with calm, calm, sweet fathomless calm. It is the Sabbath. Inhale the bouquet of Eden, the genesis of calm, exhale the exodus of balm.

283. SABBATH SURROUNDS US WITH TRANQUILITY.

I stroll along the water's edge between the sea and a sand dune hedge;

A moving speck of humanity without pride, without vanity.

Sabbath surrounds us with Tranquility.

284. ON THE SABBATH I HEAR MUSIC WRITTEN IN HEAVEN

Dear God You Composed the tranquil music in my soul

And Inscribed the lyrics that I daily unscroll

It is The Sabbath, a time to sing the music God Composes.

285. ON SABBATH REST I AM BLESSED

As I lay my head down to sleep; my body is calm and soul, serene. It is The Sabbath.

The deeds I have embroidered on my soul this week have sprouted into blessings.

286. ON THIS SABBATH I REST WITH YOU OH GOD FROM CREATION

During this week I scaled Your mountain jagged and steep, I gazed upon a majestic scene

Today is The Sabbath and I am rested, contented, fulfilled, serene.

287. ON SABBATH I PONDER THE WONDERS OF CREATION

I sit at the shrine inside my mind and ponder the wonders of Creation.

There in the midst of the safety of Your Oasis my soul is imbued with kindness.

For this is the Sabbath, an instant of sacred time.

288. ON THIS SABBATH I FEEL THE CALM OF YOUR MERCY

I Breathe in the Divine Author of Peace Who Will Proclaim calm throughout my being

And Will Make me free as I give a long Sabbath breath out

How awe-inspiring is the Sabbath, Bellweather of Eden.

289. ON THIS SABBATH I BEGIN TO MEND OIR WORLD

Dear God! You Give me Purpose and I will each day perform acts of kindness.

On this Sabbath Day I vow to take needle and thread and mend this world.

290. GOD! FREE ME TO DO GOOD WORKS

Dear God, my Refuge! My Haven! Unshackle me from my angst and I will be soothed.

Liberate me on this Sabbath to perform good works.

291.MERCIFUL GOD SHOW ME THE WAY TO EVERLASTING PEACE

God of Mercy! In my anguish I prayed to You. You Listened,

Mended my broken spirit and Wrapped me in Supreme Joy.

Praised is Your Name on this Sabbath.

292. ON SABBATH, I PRAY, YOU HELP ME REBUILD YOUR WORLD

Oh God! Hear my voice; I have worries that gnaw at the marrow of my soul I seek You, Fount of Wisdom, for enlightenment on this Sabbath Day to restore Your World as it was in Eden.

293. ON THIS SABBATH WE ARE PARTNERS IN PRESERVING CREATION

Oh God! I, a speck in Space and a tick in Time, behold Your Splendid Creation:

The Tallest Mountains, the Deepest Oceans and the Lustrous Lights of Heaven.

Who but You Can Help me? On this Sabbath we are partners in Creation.

294. ON THIS SABBATH HELP ME FIND SALVATION

Oh God! Awed am I by Your Sublime Creation,

Teach me how to earn Salvation.

295. MY SHIELD, PROTECT ME FROM SORROW

You, God, My Judge and Shield, Know my honesty, Assess me on the Divine Scale of Virtue.

This Sabbath Lift my soul out of despair.

296. GOD YOU ARE MY SHIELD

Oh God! My shield and protector. Save me from wayward ways,

297. THIS SABBATH CROWN MY SOUL WITH YOUR MAJESTY

Oh God! Cherish me. Crown my soul with Your Majesty.

298. ON THIS SABBATH I LOVE GOD WITH ALL OF MY MIGHT

I focus my Self on the quiet of my mind where I love God with all my might;

I feel the Divine Presence from the birth of day until the last instant of night.

299. ON THIS SABBATH I PRAY FOR HEALING

O God Divine! I pray Heal our wounded in body and soul.

Evict the pain and anguish that gnaws at our will.

Give affliction wings to fly away; Drop its burdens into the sea .

Command the rising swells to swallow and dissolve it until it vanishes.

With Your Divine Healing, Brighten each tomorrow.

300. ON SABBATH WE TASTE DIVINE AMBROSIA

We pray to You throughout this day and night, we pray with all our might

To Sustain our hungry, needy kin and Make us better people than we have been;

We will taste Your Love forever and I will endeavor to earn it.

Long life to all who live for the Sabbath.

Oh God Be my compass is life. I know You God.

Your Kindness is without peer; Your Mercy is sincere.

By Your strength am I awed.

On Sabbath You Give purpose to my life's quest.

On Sabbath I awake truly Blessed

By Your Divine strength am I profoundly awed.

www.ingramcontent.com/pod-product-compliance
Lightning Source LLC
LaVergne TN
LVHW021617080426
835510LV00019B/2610